FOREWARD

This is a big responsibility; a monumental undertaking. Yes, exaggerated, but, I do worry about how what you will read will come across. To a degree, I'm becoming a voice, *The* voice for T.S. women. I want to get it right; I want it to be worthy.

There are others, I'm sure, who would have given a lot more of the medical and technical side. Not that I don't believe that it's important, but, it's what's underneath that I want to relay. All the emotional, mental, and social implications of the Syndrome are what I feel needs to be brought to the surface. A coming up for air; a breath from my metaphoric lungs.

I feel a discussion on any topic surrounding Turner Syndrome is imperative for understanding and tolerance. We humans scare easily from the unknown. Most people hesitate to say they saw the proverbial pink elephant until they're certain someone else has seen it too.

That's my main reason for adding my journals and poetry. I wanted that personal connection. There's no shame in this for me – anymore. It's a part of who I am. I am a big believer that emotions are neither right nor wrong; they just *are*. They could be hateful, unfortunate, even terrifying, but if it's something you're feeling, it's valid. It is real. There is a wonderful saying by Socrates: 'an unexamined life is not worth living'. I like to think that's what I'm doing here. Maybe, just maybe, it might help others take a

look at their own.

MY STORY

I was born Mary Shirley Rosa Vallee. This is the story of my life, well, up to this point at least. My story is not unlike any other in the sense that I probably make it out to be more than what it really is. The emotions involved in writing it are more intense than its purpose. The nature of the story is my struggle, or would be struggle, to overcome the self-imposed fears and reservations that I cling to. Some of the story is told through journals and poems.

I guess it would be best for me to start at the beginning. I was born in Cornwall; a small town in Ontario, Canada, by a seemingly middle class couple. I had a toy-filled nursery, a sister, and Turner Syndrome. I was born on November 11, 1970 at 8:29 P.M. I weighed 5 pounds and 3 ounces. I was diagnosed at birth, and not given a very promising prognosis. Now, 37 years later, and only in the last decade has the situation been changing for others born with the Syndrome.

My parents were told that I might not walk, and would more than likely be *retarded*. That was in 1970, and here I am today: walking and, well, as you will read, you can't shut me up. I've also been to, and graduated from, College. Thankfully, my parents stayed strong and envisioned the best scenario instead of listening to the one they were given. I wonder sometimes what might have happened if my Mom found out early enough to have an abortion. Would the Doctor have recommended it? To this day, I have an issue with thinking that I'm not *Enough*. All those awful questions sometimes go through my mind: Do people think I'm slow? Am I intelligent? Were the doctors right? The dirtiest words in the English language to me are *stupid* and *retarded.*

 I took Behavioral Sciences in College and I remember getting so upset that I confronted the professor. The book we were using kept repeating that awful word, and it really bothered me. It got so bad, that I had to bring it to his attention. Don't think anything was done, but at least I spoke my mind. Yes, I am opinionated.

 What I recall from my childhood is the fact that my family was very protective of me, and kept me happy. I believe this affected me in the sense that even as an adult, I tend to feel the need for pampering and acceptance. Unfortunately it also means I overwhelm very easily, and I'm extremely sensitive. My beautiful husband states that I wasn't conditioned for the harshness of the real world. It's hard for me to perceive anything for myself. I need it validated. I do a lot of "Well, what do you think? Is that right? Is that okay?" I constantly second guess myself. I should explain why my parents felt compelled to guard me. Turner

Syndrome has a variety of physical traits that are part of the condition. All parents faced with that situation, I assume, would want to hide, or play down those differences so their child isn't glared at when out in public. I can't blame them for that. I am better today; well let's just say I'm a little better. It's a forever process. You adjust. Somehow you begin to *deal*. The looks from people are still there from time to time. Sometimes there are questions. I really try to see it now as a chance to maybe educate, to explain. Not always an easy endeavor.

I did enjoy the fact that my parents were involved during my childhood. They cared about what my hobbies were. They were interested in knowing who my friends were, and who their parents were, etc. I remember going out to the movies a lot. I could lose myself for two hours and forget about my life. To this day, I feel that acting is glamorous. Anyway, it was no problem to get my mom to drive me and my friends to the mall / theater. That way she knew who I was with and what I was doing.

I was crazy about Walt Disney cartoons growing up. My mom and I both, though, had a problem with Dumbo. The one scene in particular that stands out, is where Dumbo is being *abused*, picked-on etc. and the mother freaks, and commences to whipping on some mean human butt. My mom has always been protective, so it hit close to home. Dumbo being teased mercilessly because he's different. Visibly different ... I can relate. To this day, I can vividly recall a later scene where the mom, now in a cage, picks him up with her trunk, through the bars, and rocks him, soothing and comforting him. Yep, gets me every time.

I grew up like everybody else, for the most part. My schooling was unique for a while because I was mildly dyslexic. In the 2nd grade I spent mornings in a special class to correct it. It still catches me occasionally, but nothing that's stopped me from entering a work environment. In grade school my best friend was also a neighbor, so that allowed for enormous amounts of play time. Our vogue thing to do was to create massive
Barbie houses by out-lining them with string. My Father dabbles with carpentry, and made my sister and I couches, chairs, and such from wood. My Mom would help him with the upholstery.

High School was a nightmare. That might be a little embellished, but it was awkward. I had yet to *blossom*, but it was more in the sense that I didn't care about boys, except for Noah, of course. He shared my love for all things fantasy. I was a Star Wars freak, who played Coleco Vision. I totally believe that it actually helped me with spatial dexterity – a possible issue with individuals who have Turner Syndrome. I didn't party, didn't experiment with drugs or alcohol. I remember when I was maybe around 15, I wanted to stay in contact with one of my cousins who lived in Toronto. She was right around my age. We had visited them, and she had seemed so cool. She smoked, drank, etc. Why I thought that meant maturity I have no idea. When I mentioned to someone about wanting to start writing her, I got this reaction: "don't think that's a good idea, you're a little immature for her." Thank God today I just see it as staying young at heart. I'm always happy to *not* act my age.

I remember a crush I had on the boy next door. Think it was around grade 7 or 8. He was adorably cute and funny. And the energy! If I remember correctly, he took

Karate. He tried to teach me how to use num-chucks to no avail. I would help him baby-sit his younger brother a lot. We'd play with hotrod cars and anything Star Wars. Oh! And V. You know; that Science Fiction TV show? I was always the sultry Dianna, trying to tempt the poor little human rebel leader. We never did more than kiss, honest, but I recall how being in that role made me feel more attractive, more normal, more, well, female. Not that I knew all the nuances of physical attraction, but I felt I affected him, somehow. It all tied into that sense of maybe I actually belonged. Was legit. Vital.

Clothes shopping has always been an issue. My adult height is 4 foot 5 inches. Pants are worse than tops for sizing. Unless they're capris, everything has to be altered. It's easier being in Richmond, VA, though, because it never gets extremely cold. I don't have to wear *winter* pants, which helps. There are fall slacks that come in caprice styles here. If I do need something hemmed, there's a great place just a couple blocks away that does great alterations. I moved here in 2003, but more of that later.

Except for the last stubborn 10 – 15 pounds, I'm fairly happy with my shape. I find I'm a little chesty, but worry about the scarring, so I haven't seriously considered a reduction. It's just amusing when I want to buy a 2 piece set of something. I have to break it up; small pants and large top.

The hubby says I dress like a rebelling teenager. He's stated that I want to relive my carefree days through my clothes. I have no clue what dressing my age means. Everything I see that should be suitable just scares me; it makes me feel old and frumpy. Just as an example of my everyday style: jeans with embroidered flowers on them, and a t-shirt with the Tasmanian Devil on it, with the caption: Mood Swings. I've been known to wear slippers with bunnies or ladybug heads on them. My socks usually have either Marilyn Monroe or Betty Boop or animals on them as well. Ditto for sleep apparel.

Shoes are horrid to shop for. If I find a pair of sandals that actually fit, (I have short, fat, wide, feet) I'll buy like 3 pairs so I have spares for years. Pumps are out of the question. Hence, I adore the Victorian style lace-up boots.

I figured out the hair thing in College, and I never go shorter than shoulder length. Again, explanation later. I go easy on makeup. Unless it's a special event, I only wear lipstick on a daily basis. Although I occasionally pluck my eyebrows, I view them as a little bushy. I really like my nose for some reason, and my eyes. I fear shaving, as bizarre as it sounds. I have this crazy idea that if I do it too often it'll grow back in darker, thicker, courser etc … in the summer I polish my toenails. And that's probably as intimate you would ever want to get with my grooming habits.

In high school I was terrified to take gym because of the change rooms. I begged my cardiologist to give me a note so I would be exempt from it. He was such a nice man. He did it, but I had to promise not to become a couch potato. I got to take advanced English, and I remember having to read the Chrysalids, by John Wyndham. It blew me away. To think that I would have been *burned* to death at birth for being a mutant …yeah. So, anyway, that book made me think a lot. I own it, and reread it every year. Frankenstein, for its own reasons, intrigues me too.

I actually wonder if there's been any research into eating disorders and Turner Syndrome. To me, personally, there's a plausible reason for a connection. I've always been weird about food. *Always.* It's naturally harder to keep weight down the shorter you are. That's my logic, anyway. Not that I'm making excuses, but I just feel I have to watch what I eat to the last calorie. At my height even eating 1100 calories a day would probably get me in trouble. I do have asthma, so exercising isn't much *fun.* I do have to admit, though, that when I actually do get on my elliptical, I do feel better. I can't stress this enough: with all the possible health issues surrounding T.S. it's extremely important that we try to be active and eat healthy. If you have health issues, keep your doctors. busy. Make sure you get the answers you want. Protect and cherish the *Temple* that is *You.* Wow, that was preachy – sorry.

At the age of 36, I'm now beginning to feel my age – well, older actually. It started when my asthma became more of an issue. I then found out this year that my hearing is going, and that I could actually use a hearing aid. And yes, all this could be attributed to Turner Syndrome. I also have a heart murmur. Most women with T.S. have a cardiologist, pulmonary specialist (for asthma and other breathing issues) endocrinologist (for thyroid issues, and yes again, I'm on Synthroid for hypothyroidism) gynecologist, and a family Dr. Finally, just the day before I wrote this section, I found out that I flunked a bone density test. I try to be optimistic, hopeful, and grateful for the health that I do have, but – damn, I'm now questioning the old adage that you fall apart after 35. I fight by taking my vitamins, and by learning to like non-fat milk, and by constantly reminding myself I actually like using the elliptical, and eating asparagus.

I have an idea for someone with money who wants to embark on a business venture: exercise equipment for people under 5 foot 1. I would love to have a complete home gym, but a lot of the stuff just wouldn't be feasible. I'm sure there's a huge market for scaled down weight machines, rowers, abdominal machines, etc.

My sister, Rita, was patient with me as a snot-nosed toddler. She found it hard because our parents needed to give me so much attention, but I believe she cared, and obviously still does. If she resented me, I know that's behind us. I heard that I was extremely sick for the first six months of my life. I think it had something to do with my digestive system, either not being able to eat, or just not wanting to. God I wish I had that problem now! It was some gastrointestinal problem.

My parents told me that there was a massive snow storm the winter I was born. I was in the hospital at the time, and they were worried about getting stuck or stranded when coming to visit me.

Anyway, I understand why Rita might have felt neglected when I was born. Even to this day, I love being in the spotlight. I'll be the 1st to admit I love being the center of attention.

I know, when I was young, I worshipped Rita because, to me, she had attention from others, if not from our parents. She had cool friends, she was tall, and becoming very independent. Rita is also seven years older; reason enough for a pedestal I thought. I should also admire the fact that she put up with me when we played together. I had this horrible habit of telling her what her doll should be saying. I'd already have a story line in my head, along with the script. I think it just showed that I had a very active imagination. Even so, it really used to 'cheese' her. I want to be able to have that effect in my real life: Wouldn't it be wonderful to just command your life like that? "Ok I will go to my mail box and there will be an enormous check. There will be no more hunger or polluted waters. We will be able to breathe clean air. How about no more war, disease, etc…" You get the picture.

Dictating my life hasn't been easy. Anxious is the way I go through most of my days. There is so much I want for myself and my family. So much I want for this beautiful world of ours. There are things that make me feel so powerless though, and it can be terrifying. I can easily feel that loss of control. To try to abate the getting overwhelmed thing, I have become a list freak. I'm always making lists of what I need to do. It seems to help. I can see it on paper, and say "ok, that's only going to take 10 minutes, that's only going to take 15." It makes things appear manageable. Something I feel I can accomplish without yelling, screaming and crying.

I realized when I was younger that what you say can really have an affect, and not necessarily a good one. I had a really big mouth. Case in point: I was around 11, maybe younger when the incident occurred. To set the scene: my sister was sitting with my mom at the kitchen table. I join them, because I'm nosy, and I noticed that my sister has a makeup case with her. She asks if I like it, or something like that, and for some *stupid* reason I ask her why she's showing it off. I'll never forget her reaction. Her expression turned sad, well, half-sad half-pissed. In a contained voice, she replied, "I brought it over for you." I could have died. I felt awful. I apologized, but the damage was done, and this awkwardness fell over the room for awhile. To this day, I think because of that event, I'm over cautious. If I think for a second that something I say will cause any controversy at all, I'll keep quiet. I worry about how someone will react to what I tell them, not necessarily the words spoken, but the underlying meaning. I concern myself with the consequences, over-think them.

I remember one instance at school, maybe grade 4; I had broken my wrist, and being right handed, it made doing *anything* difficult. For whatever reason, I was out of the classroom, well, when I walked back in, I heard the teacher explaining it to the students. She, well, I honestly don't recall that the teacher was female; anyway, the teacher was advising them to be helpful, nice etc... Traumatic is a strong word, but, it really bothered me. Maybe it was then I first knew that people had ideas about you, that they might actually think about you. People might talk about you when you aren't even there. People might laugh, feel sorry for you, pity

you behind your back. So yeah, big, huge trust issues. How the hell do you know

something said or done is not a lie, or just part of an agenda? How do you truly

know someone loves you? Those questions haven't really diminished any.

My Father was terrific when I was young. I would sneak downstairs after

bedtime, sit on his lap and watch hockey with him. When his team would score,

he'd scream, which would make me jump then cry. I *still* don't like sudden sharp

noises. My Mom would hear us, and send me back to bed. I feel that my strength

comes from my Father. Maybe it was because he didn't want to believe that I was

different, but he never treated me that way. He taught me the importance of

education, and that knowledge holds a form of power. He knew I had intelligence,

and made me use it. He is a Korean War Veteran, and now in his 70s. He is still a

pillar of strength for me.

I have this great picture of me asleep on his lap at some wedding reception. I also

remember being around 5 and sitting in a wheelbarrow while he ran me around the

yard. I imagine how I must have been laughing and screaming as he'd break hard and make sudden turns to make me bounce around.

Our Mother is the nurturing force in the family. She's able to lick wounds a little easier than Dad. Every time I mentioned doing this project, she'd get this nervous look on her face. I think she worries about me sharing all the family secrets, and getting everybody angry with each other. My Mom tries to be there for us whenever we need her, which is quite a bit. Rita and I swear the umbilical cords are still attached! If a week goes by without us talking to each other, we wonder what we did wrong. I am now about 700 miles away from home and I get homesick often. It's hard not to feel guilty. Am I still a good daughter? Do they feel deserted? I've been reassured on a million and one different occasions that I need not worry – well, it's just what I do.

Our Mom is a friend to us. When I was still in town, we'd hang out, shop, and eat out together. The more I'm able to talk to her about me having Turner Syndrome, the closer we are. The more feedback I get on how she dealt with it, and what she felt, I understand her more. It helps me cope and feel more comfortable with it. I love our talks. I need our talks. Not all families feel that's important. Of course, we're not the average family. Sometimes I feel grateful for that.

I won't go into a tremendous detail, that would be my Mom's story, not mine. Somehow, though, I deem it warranted to state that she's a breast cancer survivor. Discovered in 2006, she has gone through the chemotherapy and radiation treatment. Her determination and resilience is amazing to me. It's wonderful when your parents both become the epitome of hope for you.

One reason, well, 2 reasons for bringing this up is that 1 - I'll be relaying a personal experience with my own breasts in a minute; and 2 - this is not just a T.S. story; to a degree, it is a Woman's story. I believe some of what I write about can pertain to any female. Regardless of anything else.

I have mixed emotions when it comes to my breasts. When I 1st developed, only with the help of hormone replacement therapy, it was shocking. I went, or so it seemed, from nothing to a healthy size B. I remember one time trying on a bathing suit, when Rita was around. I showed it to her and got an "oh my God." For some bizarre reason, I didn't see the change until then. When I did finally take notice, I was disconcerted to say the least.

Forward ahead to College; I discovered a lump. It felt completely round, a
complete circle, like one of those small neon bouncy toy balls. Not thinking much
of it, I make a Doctor's appointment. She immediately recommends a specialist.
The specialist tried to do some kind of needle biopsy and gets nothing. She
recommends day surgery to have it totally removed. I agree, still thinking it's just
a great excuse to get a day away from classes.

Rita and my mom wait it out at the hospital during the operation. Finally, I'm out
of recovery and they can see me. We wait for the results in the room, and
eventually are told that everything is fine, it's benign; nothing. Before I have a
chance to say, "Great, thank you" they start crying. Confused by their reaction, I
stupidly ask "you mean it could not have been?" Equally confused, I'm sure, the
Doctor simply states "yes." She leaves the room, and hugs abound.

If anything, I think the experience taught me not to take things for granted.

The age difference between my parents (my Dad is over 10 years older than my

Mom) has had a definite impact on me. I have only had two serious relationships before I settled down with the first man I married, and the men in both of those relationships were at least four years older than me. I know now that I was looking for someone who would take care of me, and protect me. I was looking for a father figure. I sense that's what my Mom saw in my Dad.

Since one of the purposes for writing this story is to educate, I should share some of the history of Turner Syndrome. It was discovered in the late 1930's by Dr. Henry Turner, hence the name. He was also one of the first people to study it. We humans have 23 pairs of chromosomes including a pair of sex chromosomes. Women have two X chromosomes, and men have one X and one Y. What happens with T.S. is one of the X chromosomes are either non-existent, or have been altered. This Syndrome affects roughly 1 in every 3000 females, although I've read literature that states the number is closer to 2000, or even 1500. The characteristic that is always apparent is short stature. The average adult height is 4'8". A teenager with T.S. will not develop secondary sexual characteristics, such as menstruation, breast tissue and pubic hair. The Syndrome also makes the woman infertile. With hormone therapy I'm able to menstruate, and things developed the way they should have. My first husband, Rob, said everything was in the right place anyway. The therapy starts between the ages of 10 and 12. The hormones add a slight touch of height as well. Unfortunately, the fertility problem is still present. The two options are adoption or attempting the donor eggs procedure. Thankfully, we never could decide on either.

Sometime after I started on my hormone replacement therapy, I was approached by the Children's Hospital to take part in a case study; if that's the right word. Basically this is what I was told would occur: Doctors, specialists, etc would *examine* me to gain knowledge about the Syndrome. Panel might be a good word. I think they mentioned something about tests and blood-work as well.

I might upset some people by stating truthfully that I declined. I know, and I feel like a fraud for writing all *this*. Here I am, spilling my deepest inner thoughts, sharing nearly *everything* and then blatantly refuse to get involved. I want to help, encourage and empower people to use their voice, to actively spread the knowledge and support that's so strongly needed. We need to break the silence that's still out there. But, I myself declined; said no.

Not that an explanation would justify anything, but here it goes: in retrospect I think it was the timing and my age that were contributing factors. I was in my early teens, exactly the age where no one wants to be different. Most kids at that age are dying to just fit in, avoiding anything that might alienate and isolate them. I was being asked to embrace my uniqueness. I am, to a degree, disappointed in myself, but I try to remind myself that I just wasn't at the right place at the time. As an adult I feel ready to explore the good and bad about my personality, and the Syndrome. Back then it was a new and painful territory.

There's another Turner Syndrome related medical situation that happened when I started seeing my gynecologist. Before I could really question it, he made a really endearing request. *They* wanted a picture, for medical purposes only. A reference picture depicting the physical characteristics of the Syndrome. He assured me my eyes would be blotted out, so I wouldn't be recognized, to keep my anonymity. He advised it would be a way to keep track of my development, and help specialists, Doctors, etc. have a basis for what an adolescent with Turner Syndrome looks like before therapy. He maintained it would be strictly professional, and that the photographer would show the utmost respect.

I adored Dr. Spence, and said Ok. The photographer was indeed respectful, even considerate and seemed to understand that it was delicate matter. Not that I felt dirty, but it was a bit disconcerting at the time, uncomfortable. I think that's perfectly natural. I am glad I contributed.

I think everything is different when you have a Syndrome, disease, a disorder. When there's something that takes you away from the realm of normalcy – whatever that is. Your perception of the world changes. I believe it can change the perception that the people in your world have of you as well.

I am, as of 2007, 36 years old and my perception is at a 4 foot 5 inch level. It can be surreal. My vantage point is somewhat unique. There isn't much I can see / perceive at eye level. That can be taken metaphorically as well. As an adult, I want to have conversations with adults. I am very cognizant that in every interaction I have, my height comes into play. All my physical differences affect peoples view. At least that's the association I've made. Which means it is a self-fulfilling prophecy. I'm treated like a child, therefore I throw a tantrum … I know

it puts me on the defensive. The hubby calls it the *Chihuahua Syndrome*. I bark

and make a lot of noise before anyone gets too close, trying to give the illusion I'm

big and tough.

I need to stop here for a minute and backtrack just a bit. Robert and I divorced in

2002, in our 7th year of marriage. It was a very surreal time. I spent a lot of time

crying and not sleeping. I had never had a full time job, never lived by myself, and

suddenly I had to find work, I mean *work*, and had to do a lot of growing up, and

quickly. I got my first apartment, and in a short amount of time became an official

adult. When the separation happened, I moved in with my parents. I didn't take a

lot. He kept the car and I kept the computer. I'll explain that rationale in a minute.

I had actually met someone while Rob and I were going through our worst. We

talked online innocently enough. Looking back I guess I was searching for

something more. In a way I felt it was already over. We were pretty much living

separate lives. Cliché maybe, but it was the fact at that time. It was hard to feel

guilty, it was over for me. I think for Rob too. We just didn't officially come out and say it right away.

The man I met was different from other men I'd met; besides my Dad I mean. In some ways, he's similar. No, not exploring *that* here. I will say the man I met, the man I married, taught me, and still teaches me about selflessness, compassion, about never giving up. I've learned the challenges are always going to be there, it's how you meet them that matters. He didn't, and doesn't put up with self-pity. I've found strength in him. I really needed those things at the time. And he's funny, extremely funny. Never a boring moment with him. So, sections of this book were written in the Lover's State: Virginia, where I now live.

When I first moved to the United States, we stayed with Harry's extended family. There, you now know his name! We rented the furnished basement, and shared the kitchen. It was a great arrangement because I couldn't work for about a year while I waited for my work permit.

The people we stayed with are wonderful, warm and amazing. But, I unfortunately, was a mess. I was 700 miles away from home, not able to work, worried about the whole immigration process. Not to the mention the extra stress of a new marriage.

I had never really had to deal with the concept of having in-laws, so to speak. Rob and I had never spent any real time with his family. It was difficult because I felt guilty. For some bizarre reason, I felt that if I allowed myself to get close to this woman, I would essentially be cheating on my Mom. I fear I might have done things that purposely pushed her away. Totally irrational, and it also made for a very lonely place for awhile.

I find it interesting how a person's personality can come out while playing a game. My husband and I played *Ever Quest*, it's actually how we met, and we now play *World of Warcraft*. Just to give you a bit of background to these games: basically they are online "role-playing" games. You interact with other "gamers". You're generally creating a character, killing creatures, and getting and completing quests. The reason to do all this is to get better gear and weapons and coin.

He's noticed, and so have I, that all my insecurities come out while in the game. One thing that annoys me is when another player will come along and help you kill your "mob". Most people welcome the assistance etc. I get frustrated. I, for some reason get it in my mind that the reason for them helping is that they think I can't do it myself. They're usually just being courteous, but I see it as an assault on my capabilities. My thought pattern seems to be; they're helping, so they must think I suck.

I don't take advice very well, and that really shows in the game. Part of these games is "dungeon crawling" with a group of people. The things you're killing are harder, and there's a lot more of them. Oddly enough, because of my insecurities, I play a Priest. A Priest's job is to keep everybody alive. It's a big deal. Even bigger if you can't take any criticism and take it personally if someone gives you advice. Worse, if you want to cry if someone in the group dies.

If it goes really well, I feel wonderful. If it's a bad "run" I feel incompetent, useless, and just plain dumb. From a game? Yes, from a game.

I think because when that happens it mixes in, crosses over into my real life. It's something I'm working on, but it's hard. I easily feel inadequate. These silly things start going through your mind: "My God, if I can't even play a game right …" I know, it's ridiculous, but there it is.

During my 36 years of life, I've had 4 operations, and 3 were cosmetic. The first one was on my ears. I had fairly low set ear-lobes, and the idea was to take a little off the bottom to shorten them up a little. Bad idea. The operation was a disaster. I was 4 or 5, and only given a local anesthetic. That in itself was a big mistake. I felt like I was being dissected. I had no idea what was going on, and responded by crying, kicking, and screaming. Needless to say they weren't able to finish the procedure. The operation was redone successfully when I was 14 or 15. My Mom said the Doctor had a terrible attitude, and seemed to blame her for everything. My Mom confessed to me once that for a very long time she kept wondering what she did to deserve everything she had to go through with me. She said it took her years to realize it wasn't her fault, Dad's, or mine. An important point to make about Turner Syndrome is that neither the Father nor Mother can be blamed for a T.S. birth. The loss or mutation of the X chromosome is just a random happening with the sex cells during conception, nothing more.

I decided I wanted to do something about my webbed neck, think of the Star Trek Cardassian race, when I was about 12. Because I was older, the scars are still visible. Turner Syndrome can also cause excess scar tissue (keloid formation). I wasn't expecting all the pain and the long recovery process. I was fully informed about the procedure, but I was still too naive to fully comprehend. I wonder sometimes if I would have gone through with it if I'd understood completely? Absolutely. I can recall sitting in the hospital bed when the Doctor came to remove the bandages. Actually, he brought three other nurses with him. I believe they knew what I was in for, because they removed the girl next to me from the room, and the door was closed. Because the bandages had been on for roughly three weeks, it felt like my head and shoulders had been vacuumed sealed.

When the seal was removed, there was pain. I again screamed and cried. I was so unbelievably scared. It hurt, but that's not entirely why I was crying. I'm not sure what was in the back of my mind, but pain wasn't the most prominent. It's most likely a psychological block. I've read / heard that blocks can occur in children who have experienced trauma. Think it's probably a subconscious survival technique. I do remember not wanting anyone to see me until the second set of bandages came off. I spent in total, roughly 6 or 7 weeks completely isolated from my friends. . The operation was done during the summer at "CHEO", The Children's Hospital of Eastern Ontario, so I didn't have to worry about school. I know it was the summer before I started high school. Eating and sleeping were difficult. Most nights I slept on a recliner in the living room. The last dressing came off better than the first. Our shower didn't work at the time, and I wanted more than a bath, so I used my grandmother's. The shower felt wonderful. It was great to wash my hair and around my shoulders. I felt so much lighter too after losing the weight of the bandages. I was laughing and crying all at once. Looking in the mirror, and seeing a normally shaped neck was a rebirth of sorts for me. I felt free, and more like a human being. All of a sudden, I wasn't so different and alone. There's scarring, some physical, some emotional, but I can deal with that.

The other physical aspects of Turner Syndrome that I, well, endure, are a very low hairline. The hubby shaves it for me; otherwise it would be unbearable in the summer. I have the puffy feet; thankfully the swelling in my hands went down. Don't know the technical terms, but I have the permanently bent pinkie finger on my left hand, and the 2nd to last toe, again on the left side, is a lot smaller than the baby toe. Other than that, features are basically normal; although I'd love a fuller top lip. Oh! I also don't have that little indent under the nose.

As I mentioned before, a couple of years later, I wanted my ears pulled back and snipped a little. This was a simpler operation, and easier on me, because this time I actually understood what would occur. It was funny because I had 2 holes in each ear, and after the operation, I was back to wearing only 1 set of earrings.

In the spring of '89 there was a Turner Syndrome Conference in Ottawa, Ontario. These conferences are held so that families who are dealing with the Syndrome can share thoughts, and get some feedback and information on what's happening medically. My Mom and I decided it was time for us to learn more, and create a support system. It was an excellent experience, and one I'll have for a long time. I learned that this wasn't only happening to me. Suddenly it was all right to have this Syndrome and acknowledge it. I no longer needed to hide it. The Hotel we were staying at was attached to a shopping mall, and that proved to be a bonus. If the seminars got too much for us to handle, we'd just go shopping. We did a lot of shopping. There was a main seminar where Turner Syndrome was fully explained, and the latest theories tossed around. The panel was made up of professionals who had dedicated a lot of time into researching the Syndrome. My gynecologist was one of the speakers in the panel. I was excited because his mentor, a Dr. from England, who had taught him, was a special guest. This man knew his stuff. My Mom and I learned a lot, but it was honestly overwhelming. We didn't prepare ourselves for the things we discovered about each other. We both held back because the emotions were so strong and new. Neither one of us was sure what we were suppose to do with them.

It's difficult to describe what I went through during puberty. I believe I went through it without really knowing it. I never had an acne problem, and I never thought about sex until I was roughly 17. I wasn't overly freaked out about growing breasts or menstruating, but the fact I needed to take pills to do it was unsettling. It sounds sad now, but I never had the normal concerns about becoming a woman, because I never thought I would become one. I struggle with that everyday. I think when a teenage girl realizes that her body can create another human being, something happens. I think it might instill the idea of responsibility and maturity. That wasn't there for me, because right from becoming a teenager I knew that I couldn't conceive a child. I'm sure there is more to being a woman than just being able to have a baby, but one has to admit it is a major part. Not that I was promiscuous, but I always felt I had to explain my physical situation to the person I was becoming intimate with. The questions were going to be there, I just wanted to bring them up 1st. I guess it's like laughing at yourself before someone else does ...

During high school, I wasn't really concerned with that aspect of my future, so I never gave it a lot of thought. Marriage and children weren't strong dreams in my mind. As I got older, and eventually started dating, I found myself thinking about those things a lot more. There is certain emptiness in knowing that you won't raise a family. I honestly believe that I don't want to have a child right now, but for some reason I feel it's my duty to want one. Maybe it's because it's a decision I can't make on my own. The choice was already made for me. I know my anger and resentment comes from the fact that I'll never have the option. Harry is wonderful, and sensitive to that fact that I'm, well, sensitive. He comforts me when I get overwhelmed with everything. I am blown away with his intuition. How in tune he is with me.

There are some things that no matter how much empathy you can generate, it's still impossible to understand. You just can't say to a cancer or aids victim: "I know how you feel." Unless you have cancer or aids, you don't know how that person feels. I don't wish to sound cold, and I guess it's just a case of wishing to express the encouragement of active listening. You can hear what people say, but it takes more effort to really listen to the emotions being expressed in those words. This is where the T.S. Society has been wonderful. I almost instantly felt like I had known these women for years. They are very willing to listen, and be there to lend the support that's needed. Obviously, these women realize a great deal of the struggles, and barriers that are faced by all women with Turner Syndrome. Kudos ladies. Kudos.

I hate days where I don't have people around me. I usually end up walking around the apartment aimlessly. I take time to stare out the window and watch everybody getting on with their lives, then it's back to just walking around. It's on these days where I get really philosophical about my own life. I've developed an attitude, and I'm afraid it's not a very positive one. It's wrong to feel that you're owed something. It's even worse to try to collect what you think should be yours. Do I feel the world owes me? Sometimes I feel I should get things handed to me on a silver platter. I remind myself that there is no perfect life. I'm afraid of becoming resentful, selfish, and demanding. The people who see this try not to accommodate me. I value that they care enough about me to tell me where to go. I don't want people saying "all right, I feel sorry for her, I'll do this for her." I never ask for pity. Servitude yes, pity no. Just incase it needs explaining, that was just a bad attempt at humor.

I wonder if a lot of women with T.S. feel younger than they actually are? I know

I deal with that a lot. Because of the short stature, it's probably natural for people

to want to treat me differently. I know I respond to that by sometimes acting

younger. I learned in psychology that there are 3 ways that people relate to other

people: adult to adult, child to adult, and child to child.   Being 36, I naturally want

to deal with adults on an adult to adult basis, but sometimes I feel I'm treated like

someone who needs protection and guidance. I realize that some of my actions

play a part in how people might see me. I know I don't always act as mature as I

could or should. I suppose it's a which happened first sort of circumstance. It can

be a vicious circle, and a tough one to escape. I tend to remind myself of my age,

and the fact that I'm a woman if I'm in an intimidating situation. I have a perfect

example of me not dealing with someone on an adult to adult level. I was at my

hairdressers' on a seemingly normal day, and one of her friends stopped by to see

her. Without even acknowledging me, she turned to my hairdresser and said "Why

is it whenever I come in here, you're doing a kids hair?" It seemed innocent

SHIRLEY HITER 36

enough, but being 22 at the time, I questioned her eye sight. My hairdresser looked at me, and then politely proceeded to explain to her friend that I wasn't a child. Her friend then apologized. I wanted to say "Well, I'm sure you feel pretty stupid right now, so no harm done." What I said was, "That's all right." I had a brilliant come back, and all that came out of my thin little lips was "all right"!? I seldom act on what I think simultaneously. I suppose for the rest of the world that's a good thing.

There are some things that are said that stay with you forever. Memory / perception is an amazing thing. I don't know if it's a combination of who is speaking, the words, or if it's our interpretation, our verbal digestion of those words. I can recall a couple occasion where people have left their mark with me. Once, was as a young teenager. The rural road we lived on had some great ponds that would freeze over in the winter. I've always loved skating, so it made for countless hours after school of *practicing* some spins, twirls, etc. One pond happened to be across the road from a convenience store. One night, after messing around for awhile, I decided to get some candy and head home. When I went to pay, the clerk starting commenting, stating he had seen me. At first I was really embarrassed. Although I don't remember the exact words, he was surprisingly encouraging. That much I do remember. I know it isn't a lot, but, it stayed with me. The simple fact that someone pointed out that I was *Ok* at something, that with practice I could be really good. Funny where hope can come from.

The one of the many people who I'm sure has affected me was a College professor. As a psychology teacher, she gave a couple sessions to each of the students as part of the course. She was a little dynamo. She was tiny, spunky and my God she was smart. I was in love, I swear! She was such an inspiration for so many reasons. During one of my sessions with her, we started talking about my writing and what brought me to wanting a career in social services. I didn't have a real answer, as I remember. The conversation kept coming around to my writing. She stated that I had a book "in there" and she looked forward to reading it some day. Yeah, ok. So, of course I started hounding her. I do that if you encourage me, be careful. I kept repeating, "you think so? Isn't it like impossible to get published?" I never considered that I could do something so, well, to me at least, so grandiose. It seemed so exotic, larger than life, surreal. Could it really be something I could accomplish? Those words from her really made me think about it, seriously think about it. Why not? Why not me? Writers don't have to be beautiful, athletic, or even tall. It was perfect! What was best is that I loved it. I love writing, love words. I think my absolute favorite writer for poetic value is Mary Shelly. I have recently reread Frankenstein, and as always I was blown away with her command of the language. The writing flows so beautifully, and her choice of words are just brilliant, and well, yes, poetic. In grade school I got jealous because in an English class that a friend was taking, she had to read pages of the dictionary each night. I wanted to be in that class. Writing, I felt, was something I could do, a skill I could hone.

I'm honestly not a very trusting person. If I do get close to someone, it's because I've discovered there's something I can learn from them. I don't just hang around people who are fun to be with; they have to hit a nerve with me. I hold on to my secrets tightly, and reveal them sparingly, and for a price. When I confide in someone, it's only after a strong bond has been established. This kind of trust takes a long time to build. I test people by telling them fairly trivial stuff first, then if they pass, I can move on to something more personal. I was taught growing

up, that people will use other people if they can get away with it. I guess the fact

that I grew up in the country has something to do with it. Everybody knew

everybody's business. You didn't have a secret unless you didn't speak. I fear

being vulnerable, so I've constructed a wall around myself to keep the bad people

out. Sometimes you can accidentally keep the good people away too. My frequent

uneasiness has built a barrier between me and self assurance. My performance at

work, the relationship I had with Rob, and the one I now have with Harry. Also

adding the family to that, it keeps life keeps getting harder and harder to cope with.

Being neurotic isn't a word that most people want to associate with themselves, but

I suppose I do have these tendencies. I don't know what area of my life to use to

regain control. Do I build up my confidence at work, or do I make my marriage

the best of Earth? Maybe I could finally become responsible to a degree so that

my parents will be able to sleep at night.

One of my bosses once told me that I read too much into things, and now I

understand what he was telling me. I'm always on the defensive. I generally feel that people have a hidden agenda when they interact with me. I feel that if I can remain of the defensive, I will be able to avoid any personal attack. Like Harry has said: the Chihuahua Syndrome. Close family and friends say I can be overly sensitive. My emotions are right near the surface. I seem to have this heighten awareness of emotional pain. It's almost like a telepathic power. Understanding physical pain isn't as easy, but emotional pain rips right through me. This might be the reason why I have trouble with assertiveness. I don't like confrontation. I want that gift of saying what I feel, and not being afraid to face the consequences. I know if I could just say what I feel I'd be more easily understood. Rob told me that my writing says more about me that when he had tried to talk to me about personal things. This is an easier way to express myself.

I've been finding that the more I comfort people, the more I could use it myself. I love being able to help someone, but it's sometimes tough to find empathy when I need it in return. An old high school friend phoned me remembering it was my birthday. That part was really sweet. She told me that she was depressed, so I asked her to talk to me about it. It seemed like the perfect opportunity to use my psyche training. Anyway, things were fine until she explained her dilemma. She wants another baby, and her husband doesn't. She has two beautiful girls, and she wants another baby. I could relate to the fact that at the end of each month when I get my period I cry. Bleeding is just further confirmation that I'll never have children. The irony is that I need birth control pills to even menstruate isn't lost on me. My friend needed me to understand how having two children isn't enough. Help! I don't know how to do that. The best I could do was to suggest that she concentrate on her girls. By being more involved with them, that feeling of needing another child might subside.

This may also cause her to become more resentful and withdrawn, and possibly lead to a deeper depression. But hey, the advice was free! Honestly, I do see where I'm partially responsible too. If I expect people to be sensitive to me, I need to share the things that I consider to be sensitive issues for me. My feelings are as legitimate as everybody else's, and I can own up to those feelings.

My parents let me grow up without too much trouble or interference. I owe them a lot. With all the complications I had to deal with as a baby, and the fact that even now I'm somewhat needy. I know my parents handled everything the best way they could. They endured, and continued to give me what I needed. I truly believe that I'm blessed.

I finally decided that I was an adult and needed a drivers license when I was 19. That emotional delay again … My Mom gave me a couple lessons, but, bless her, shes isn't the most patient person. I don't blame her though. I'm sure I could have made Mother Theresa want a beer. Anyway, we went through the local phonebook, and found a private instructor. He, thankfully, had patience beyond comprehension. He was friendly and encouraging, and I think we got along fine. At least I got along with him and was grateful he took me on. I really don't have much indication of how he felt about teaching me.

In the end it took a 2nd try to pass the driving / practical part of the test. It was wonderful, and it really gave me a sense of freedom. The parents were great about lending out the car for the most part, too.

There was a great woman I met at the T.S. conference I had gone to, and we kept in touch for a couple years after that. She had the use of a relatives' cottage in a little town about a 3 hours drive from Cornwall. For a couple years in a row, we used it as a retreat spot. I had the most amazing time. Starting with the ride there, the whole trip was just so liberating. I had never, on my own, traveled any great distance. And the simple fact that it took a lot of work to get there. Because of my height, I had to get past the fear that I could even get my license. To be comfortable driving in a vehicle, I need to use a cushion under my butt, and have the seat pushed all the way up and in. Not that I embarrass easily anymore, but it always causes conversation if I have someone else in the car with me, which I don't like doing. I trust my driving, but I honestly do get nervous knowing someone's safety is in my hands.

Speaking of safety: airbags. They are a marvelous invention, and yes, they do save lives. They save lives unless you're built like a 12 year old, and are nearly sitting on top of the steering wheel; then they can decapitate you. Harry and I went through a lot of telephone calls and expense when we bought our Cavalier. Being a 2004 vehicle the airbags were standard. I called the most logical place, I thought, first; the dealership. They had no information to give me on who to contact, and wouldn't deactivate the airbags themselves. Liability. I wasn't impressed with the lack of assistance though, I mean you would have thought I was the only person to ever enquire about deactivating an airbag. We did end up finding a private company who would do driver's side only. The woman who showed up to do it; graciously they come to you, said her reason for getting into the business is the fact that her mother was killed by a deploying airbag. I couldn't imagine losing someone like that. I feel it really shows quality of character that she selflessly gives now to help ensure no one else goes through the same devastating experience.

Back to the retreat: we would all contribute food for a big feast, and eat while gabbing and laughing and sipping wine. It was just a perfect setting and opportunity to talk and talk about all our issues and conflicting emotions and hopefully get some support. Also it was a chance to get all the questions answered, well, maybe not answered, but at least in the open. We realized we had all the same concerns and desires for our lives. It was, for me at least, a kinship that was created, and I miss it terribly. I need to let my guard down a little bit and try to get some connection started here.

I've learned maturity comes from caring and appreciating the good things around you. Unfortunately, there's not too much I give a shit about. My husband, immediate family, and my faith are the extent of my loyalties. I suppose you could say I'm in a state of apathy. Now there is something more that gives me a feeling of pride: my writing.

I was born and, well, raised Catholic. The grade school I attended, Sacred Heart, was Catholic. I was transfixed with religion growing up. It was just so magical to me. At the height of my reverence, I contemplated becoming a Nun. Seriously. They were called to a higher purpose, above all our petty wanting. I wanted that for myself.

I went through my First Communion, and Confirmation, reading the Bible and praying. I have to admit some of the prayers were selfish, but, in my defense, I was young. I remember praying to be taller. It was a very strange time for me.

My family weren't big Church goers, but supported me. I had a couple friends whose family would take me with them whenever I asked. I still have faith, but, sometimes it's hard. It can be hard to keep finding things to hang onto. Religion was on of the things that tore Rob and I apart, so I'm a little more leery now. More cautious.

Since I started this project, there's been a strong sense of meaning in my life. Strange, but it seems like forever that I've had this idea in my mind. Sharing my story is something I've always thought of doing. I am grateful that it came to be. I believe there's an internal battle that takes place inside everyone. Respect, accomplishments, and intellect are all things we humans crave, and sometimes even demand. For some people, this task is easily completed, but for others it's never attained. I guess that's the chip I lug around on my shoulders. Except for when I was a child, I can't remember a time where I haven't felt that I didn't need to prove myself. Wanting to be seen as someone with something to offer is common, but because of my stature (or lack of it), I feel like I've had to surpass expectations in order to believe I'm capable.

Growing up, though, I went by the assumption that no one expected anything from me. For the longest time, it made things immensely easy for me. There wasn't any goal setting and the fretting about it afterwards. No performance anxiety of any sort. I had a very pressure free existence. I don't know when it happened, but I started to believe it was self pity that made me want to hide, that made it easier to just not try. If I tried, I could possibly fail. I hated the thought of worrying how long the list would be of things that I couldn't do. Somehow an excruciating slow process began, and the self pity went away, or at least enough of it, and I able to start envisioning things for myself. I also found that most of my limitations are self imposed. I discovered I didn't want those limitations anymore. I allowed myself to grow up, and become a woman - hear me roar!

Harry and I will celebrate our 4th anniversary on October 28th. There was some cosmic happening that occurred when we met. I almost instantly trusted him. I could tell him about the Syndrome, and knew that he wouldn't run away. Ten years ago, I don't think I was imagining this. It's something I never thought about. I was the kind of child who felt they would live at home forever. I know my parents are happy that I found someone who is good to me, cares, and respects me. We joke and say that the only reason we're perfectly matched is because no one else would have us. It hasn't always been easy. We have our little tiffs like all couples. We are dealing with something a little different though because of me having T.S. We know that we are going to see each other through any situation. Harry and I feel we give to each other something that would otherwise be missing. He'd never want me to get too personal, but I believe I know how he feels. He's learned that it's important to care for someone, and to know you're cared for in return. Even if that vulnerability terrifies you. I've learned about unconditional love. It doesn't matter what my thoughts are, I can share them. I'm not scared of who I am when I'm with him. I can share anything without the fear of losing him. It's ironic in a way. It's because of his influence in my life, that I've become independent and self respectful. I love him dearly, but I know I would be all right on my own.

I think it's important for women with T.S. to know they can fulfill their own needs. You don't need someone else to validate your importance. Harry supports me in my endeavors, but I know it's my own desire that will motivate me to achieve my dreams.

I had put my need to nurture into two adopted cats. "Boo" was born on March 11, 1995. We had him since April of 1996. He is basically your typical fat cat, but with gorgeous white fur. "Sable" is the sophisticated female. She was roughly six years old at the time. Her Siamese features are a real contrast to Boo's rotund body. Rob adored them almost as much as I did. When you allow a butt to be 3 inches away from your face while you sleep, it's love. I think a lot about how I've been able to grow into a fairly together adult has to deal with the responsibility I had to Rob and the cats. When Rob and I separated, the cats went to his parents. Around my 35 birthday, Harry and I got Ling, a traditional Siamese. She'll be 2 in August, and is an absolute joy.

SHIRLEY HITER 50

With Harry I'm forced to deal with him on an adult to adult level. I'm a woman to him, and his wife. Our precious cat, Ling, teaches me patience and nurturing. Sometimes I get a little overwhelmed. I think about my possible career choices, all the decisions I never considered making are right in front of me now. When I realized that I was handling the high school experience, it opened doors for me. I was suddenly seeing myself as a smart and capable person. I could think about Colleges, and I did. I have a diploma in social services (behavioral sciences). I also worked on a diploma in accounting. I knew I could have a career, and even romantic involvements. I can take care of myself, and make intelligent choices for myself. I deserve to live my life for me, and the things that are important to me, namely my husband, family, and happiness.

If there is one last thing I get to ever say about what I have written, it is a favor I need to ask any parent or guardian of a girl with Turner Syndrome. Please don't hide them. Let them learn and experience life. They can achieve as much, or even more than anyone else. Give them the opportunities to shine, and they will.

Thank you for reading, and I hope you have enjoyed it. I certainly have enjoyed writing it. From the bottom of my heart, I thank you.

This section is a collection of my journals. They are important because I can use them to vent certain emotions, and to keep in check all the millions of different feelings I seem to experience all at once. These specific ones deal with the harder aspects of my growing up. Because these journals are very open, some of the content might not be suitable for young readers. Parents might want to flip through them themselves before allowing a young person to read them.

JOURNAL Dec. 1980

Nothing exciting happened today. I broke my wrist, and while I was at the
hospital I found out I have something called Turner Syndrome. I guess my mom
thought I knew, or was waiting for a good time. I just turned ten, and I've had it
since birth. A good time?

I know I'm different, but I was hoping to be different in the same way that
everybody is different. Fat chance. I'm one in every three thousand females
different. My mom said something about seeing a special Dr. in Ottawa. Someone
who sees a lot of girls like me. Maybe he can give me addresses, because I'm the
first one I've ever known. I wonder if I'll ever meet and become friends with
someone who has T.S.?   I don't feel like writing anymore, so bye.

JOURNAL   May 1990

I just had a talk with my mom, and it was something out of a sitcom. Mom was in her bedroom, and I was really upset, so I went to say hi and stuff. I didn't stay long and went back to my room. She obviously knew something was wrong, and asked me about it. I sat on my bed, and started to cry. I mean really cry. I told her about how Dan and I are thinking about having sex. I still can't believe I told her. I told her how scared, angry, and confused I am. I look all right dressed, but what if I'm hideous nude, and that leads into how much I tell him about having T.S. Do I explain I can't have children? Do I show him my scars? Do I point out all my abnormalities in-case he notices and asks questions? The anger comes from the fact that I don't need this shit. I don't want to deal with these things. I resent having to. If I share my thoughts, who's going to understand? Anyway, my mom handled it perfectly, and I feel better now. I'll become kinky, and make him wear a blindfold. Ha, ha.

JOURNAL

I had a counseling session with my Psyche. teacher today. I'm comfortable talking to her, but it doesn't make it easier. It's all right to have a problem, but I don't want her thinking I need to be committed or anything. That's why I don't usually share things with people. I don't know how much to divulge.

Dan is being a real jerk! I got dates mixed up on something we were supposed to do, and apparently the creep wanted to go hunting on the same day. I hate hunting! How can I be with a man who hunts? He accused me of spoiling all his fun. To teach me a lesson, he refused to go with me, and spent his weekend with the guys. I really don't think this will last. I've worked too hard to see myself as an adult, he's not going to treat me like a child! Yet, I'm still afraid to let go. There's still a part of me that cares for the SOB. Do I have the energy to start over? I feel like I confessed so much. Too many things were shared to quit now. What to do...I need to stop living, half denying that I have T.S. Shit, I still have trouble spelling the whole thing out! Let's try it: Turner Syndrome There, I feel reborn. Goodnight.

AMAZING JOURNAL Dec 19th 1991

I am so excited. I met someone at work tonight. We talked for an hour! His name is Rob, and he's so sweet. I think he likes me to. We have a date set for tomorrow night after I finish work. He's sort of sexy too. He's a little shy, but I can work on him. Ha,

This is some early Christmas gift. Good Night.

SAD JOURNAL April 30th 1992

My Grandmother died yesterday. Mrs. Madeline Merpaw. I was at the College, and Rita's husband Alan picked me up and drove me to the hospital. When I arrived, all I could do was tell her I was there, and try to hold her hand. It was tough because her breathing was so irregular and raspy. Part of me wanted to run away. I just keptsaying who I was and that I was there, and it was all right. What was all right? The fact that she was dying? Close family think she waited for me, because ten minutes after I got there, she died. Part of me thinks that if I didn't go into her room, she'd be alive today. I know that's not how it works. I'm glad she let me say goodbye. Rob said he'll go to the wake and funeral. He'll be great through this. I know he will. Anyway, the house is starting to fill up again, I better go. Thanks for listening.

JOURNAL

Rob and I stared into each other's eyes today and professed our love for each other. Corny huh? Anyway, it looks like we're going to move in together. We talked about it a lot. This isn't just for fun. We know it means forever. One day we will be married. Married. The word seems so strange. Someone wants to be with me! With all my little quirks, and anxieties! Someone wants to be with me. I know how terrible it sounds, but I never thought I would get married. I didn't know how I would find someone to care about me. I wasn't expecting any-one to get past the fact I have T.S. I know my parents love me, but I think parents have to love their kids, no matter what. Rob sees me as a person with the same kind of struggles as everybody else. He loves my laugh, he says I can be genuinely sexy. There is nothing fake about it. He's attracted to me, all of me. The scars don't matter, the puffy feet don't matter, and the fact that I can't have children is something he's ready to deal with. He told me he's not with me specifically to have kids anyway. He means a lot to me. He's willing to deal with whatever we need to. The commitment is ready to be made, actually it already has.

DEAR JOURNAL May 18th 1992

I gave my mom quite the scare today. I woke up extremely early and caught the first bus to Rob's. We had apartments to look at! Anyway, I forgot to leave a note, so when she got up to go to work, I wasn't home. She assumed that I had gone jogging, per usual. When I wasn't home by the time she was ready to leave, she freaked. I can't believe I had my mother thinking I was attacked and probably left for dead. My mom called Rob's, but we were celebrating our decision to live together, in the bedroom, so we didn't hear the phone. Just when we were about to leave, my dad knocked at the door. I knew instantly he knew what happened. My father knows everything. He was just happy to see that I was O.K., but told me what my mom went through. I phoned right away. She was still crying. I felt just awful. Rob and I were finally able to apartment hunt. We fell in love with the first place we saw. A spacious two bedroom on ground level. It's beautiful. The great news is we can move in July 1st! I got the call about an hour ago. I need to suck up now. I'm going to apologize again, and watch TV with my mom. Good night.

SHIRLEY HITER 60

JOURNAL

I feel like I'm always solving everybody's problem. Today it was Carrie. She's not happy she says, she wants a man she says, she hates her parents she says. Well, who the hell has a monopoly on happiness? Maybe I carry around this cheery attitude or something. Maybe, because I don't bother people with my garbage, they assume I must be happy? My life stinks just as much as everyone else's. I'm not a great problem solver, so why do I play shrink for everyone? I'm sure most people feel people dump their problems on them. I told Carrie we could go out tonight, and get her mind off things. She had no problem going out, but I was warned not to invite Cindy. It's funny, nobody likes Cindy. I agreed, and as soon as we hung up I called Cindy to tell her to meet us there. I'm such a bitch! If anything exciting happens, I'll let you know.

JOURNAL

My mom and I had an interesting talk about our personalities today. She heard that a person's character is developed between the ages of 6 and 12, and she wanted my thoughts. I told her Freud (I love Freud) believed this happened by the time the child was 5. She wanted some examples from my childhood to support the theory. I think the most prominent is my fear of confrontation. I've always been a coward when there's yelling, screaming, or insults involved. Any kind of violence makes me ill. I can remember when I was really young, if my dad yelled at my sister, I would cry. It wasn't directed at me, but it would still bring tears to my eyes. It's like a strange fear of being condemned or criticized. I feel it may be the little girl in me who wants to make everybody proud, and who doesn't want to do anything wrong. It could also be the part of me that's a spoiled brat who craves attention. The kind of person that cries when they don't get their way. Maybe I feel the world owes me, what's it to you anyway?

JOURNAL

A very sad entry. Today my mom and I were talking, and my birth came up for some reason. She said that for a long time, she wondered what she did to deserve me, because of all the sickness I went through during the first year. The news almost made me sick to my stomach. I'm glad she was able to talk to me about it, and I know she obviously no longer feels that way. I know she hasn't felt that way in an extremely long time. Somehow just knowing about it makes me feel hurt, angry, and guilty. I'm hurt because there was a time when she found it tough to care. Angry, because I was a baby for crying out loud! It wasn't my fault. I know the real reason for her feeling that way is because deep down my mom and dad feel responsible for me having T.S., so there's a tinge of guilt. Turner's Syndrome is something that can't be predicted. There's no way of knowing that it's going to occur. To date, it still can't be prevented. It's something that can happen to any couple, no matter who the two people are. No blame can go to anyone. Maybe I never told them that. What if my parents don't know that I don't blame them? How do you say something like that face to face without falling apart? As much as

I might need to, I don't have the courage or strength to say it. I hope writing it will do.

Mom, dad I need you to know that I will never blame you or feel you're responsible. No other parents could have cared for me, and treated me with so much love when I needed you both. That is why God gave me to you to be nurtured and raised. No two people on Earth could have done a better job. I owe you everything. Love Babe. I know they might never read it, or I might never be able to say it, but writing assures me that I feel it.

JOURNAL Aug. 1994

I've been thinking about having children again. As much as I know it's impossible, I want to believe there's a chance. Part of me thinks I would make a wonderful mother. Part of me thinks there has to be some reason why I can't. Other than physical I mean. Maybe I shouldn't be a parent, and this was the best way to ensure that I didn't. You know, maybe someone knows something I don't. I hate seeing diaper commercials, or talk shows about the wonders of parenting. It was fine when I was single, but now that I'm married, and getting older, I feel the need to start a family. Adoption is a great option, but I want to child to be mine, and even if I got the baby an hour after birth, I know it wouldn't be completely mine. I hear so much about the experiences of carrying a baby, and delivering, and a lot of it is good stuff. It's almost impossible to talk to friends who have children, because naturally they want to share all the cute stories about their kids. Sometimes they're really enjoyable to listen to, and sometimes they can be heart wrenching. Anyway, it is late, and I'm tired. Bye.

JOURNAL March 17th 1995

I just had a horrible dream. I dreamt I had a baby girl, but that's not the bad part.
The baby kept saying "are you short mommy? Are you a woman mommy?" After
listening and staring blankly at the child, I nuked her. I microwaved her! I woke
up when the microwave beeped. The beep turned out to be a car horn, which was
what woke me up. I know exactly why this happened. I was in the bank yesterday,
and while I was in line this kid was staring at me. The child began asking me if I
was short. Not in a whisper, it was loud enough for heads to turn. The question
wasn't asked once, but a few times over. I wanted to tell her "No, it's an illusion.
I'm actually 5'10', and blond." Instead I froze, and said nothing. I turned my head
and silently begged her to stop. I know, Wimp! By the time the mother
intervened, I was humiliated. Stuff like this ruins you for the whole day. You're
the only one that knows. It would just feel too weird telling anyone who would be
able to respond.

DEAR JOURNAL

I was keeping for my sister last night. Megan is beautiful. She's only three months old, and still delicate. When she woke up from her nap, I decided to hold her for a little while. This feeling of jealousy and despair came over me, and I started to cry. I just kept thinking of not being able to have one of my own. It overwhelmed me. It scared me actually. It had never come over me that strongly before. I let myself cry. I still had a couple of hours before they came home, so I just let myself cry. I was better afterward, and much more together. I know I need to deal with it day by day. Like everything else, some days will be easier than other's.

JOURNAL

I went on the web last night and checked out the T.S. sites. They were very informative. I'm surprised there isn't a lot of Canadian content though. Anyway, I put my name on a list where women who have the Syndrome can send E-mail to each other. I took someone's address right away, and added my name to the list. I hope the response is good. It would be really nice to connect with other women who are experiencing the some sort of things that I am. It will be a great support system. See ya.

These journals work a little different. These following entries were actually part of

an online Blog from Bravenet.com. Enjoy!

Ugh! Well, looks like I have a bit of insomnia. *yawns* I am so happy to have

both Sites to keep me busy, but, I think that's the problem, I can't shut my mind off

when it's time for bed. I've always been like this. For as long as I can remember, I

hated to sleep if I thought there was something better going on. What's worse, is

Harry wants to go out when he gets home from work in a couple hrs. He needs

snacks for work, and I need my Diet Pepsi *grins* My Sisters bday is coming up,

so I need to take care of that, too.

 Going through some old papers I found some more poems. Yay! I need to do

some final primping on them to make sure they're Site worthy. *giggles* Oh! Not

all poems are going to be placed on this Site, some will now go to

Shirleyonline.com, so if you've liked my Poems, feel free to check it out now and

then. *yawns* Well, tks for reading my ramblings, and don't forget: Thurs at

3:30pm Est, and Sun at 6:30pm EST Ciao!

Shirley ... March 17th 2004 ... 4:30am EST.

Hullos! Looking like the cooler weather has hit us. There was a major thunder /

lightning storm here last night, and we woke up with it being at least 10 degrees

less than what it had been during the week.

Hubby took me to the Cracker Barrel on Saturday. Great Southern style food and a

very pleasant atmosphere. Sunday we got together with his family for something

called: Soup Sunday. Family gets together to sample homemade soups. Even

with making sure my portions were tiny, I didn't get around to everyone's, but

what I did have was wonderful.

The news we've all been waiting for: *drum rolls* www.shirleyonline.com is

Live! Yay! Until the networking thing really starts happening things are going to

be slow, so I've been doing what I can to try to help it along. It takes forever for

search engines to "crawl" and find the URL, so I've joined a couple Writers groups,

and emailed a few people to exchange Links. I'm hoping within a couple weeks

things will start to happen with it. I've been told, I'm not the most patient person,

though. Things should have happened yesterday, is kinda my philosophy. *grins*

I want to thank everyone for being so supportive during this little endeavor. It

means alot.

Have a great week, Ya'll!

Shirley ... March 8th 2004 ... 3:15pm EST

Wow! Nothing like walking in the fresh air with Madonnain the discman, to make one appreciate life. hahaha It got into the 70s here today, I'm sure. I was in a no neck, and short sleeved shirt, and I was nearly sweating. Sorry, perspiring; I am a lady, I'll have ya'll know. *grins*

I am close to bringing the other Site online. Just the final primping of the stories, and the Site itself.

Sister had icky Dr's appointment, and needs more tests done, so, please, again, send good thoughts this way. I'll make sure to relay them to her. *grins*

We're closer to getting the paperwork mailed out, so I can become a permanent resident, and finally get working. The stuff we needed to gather beforehand was unreal, not to mention the money needed for processing. Did I mention that each form has its own processing fee? *rolls eyes* Except for my writing, I don't aspire to much, career wise, so my dream job would be working in a quiet book store. Hubby said there are writing guilds all over the city, and one must be dedicated to fantasy. Will probably head to the bookstore soon, and check out the bulletin boards. I'm wondering about magazine work, too, but it's a catch 22 .. how much experience do I need before I can gain some experience. *giggles*

SHIRLEY HITER 73

Anyway, I've rambled on long enough. Oh, and as a P.S. There is a 2nd Chat time starting up: Thurs afternoon at 3:30 pm EST. Hope to see people there. Happy hump day!

Shirley ... March 3rd 2004 ... Approx 2:10pm EST

Update on Mam and Ultrasound Appt, which was today ...Going to make this fairly brief ... Although, I still have a consultation with the Dr tomorrow, from what they could tell, they only need to see me in 6 Months. Then they can check to see if theres a difference. I was told it's normal seeing as I'm a new patient. If there's a change, they will have something to go by I suppose. The tests were about what I expected. The highligh was getting to wear a *pastey* over my nipples. I joked that I felt like Janet at the Super Bowl. That got a few laughs. *Grins*

And thank you, I did feel all those good thoughts. *Smiles*

Shirley ... Tues, Feb 17th 2004 ... Late for me; 8:15pm EST

Just woke up, so writing this while still a big groggy, so, you'll have to forgive me. Diet Pepsi already in hand, so, should be caffeinated shortly ... Never acquired a taste for hot drinks. Mug of hot chocolate on Christmas morning, but, that's about it. I think it's because you have to drink them fast for them to taste ok ... I can nurse a soft drink for like 2 hrs. Try making a coffee last that long. ICK!***grins***

Well, good news and bad news ... Good news is that I finally went to see a gynochologist <spelling>, the bad news is that she found uhmmm abnormal tissue, while doing the breast exam thing.

She was none to gentle about it either ... Ouch! ***grins*** anyway, I have to now have an ulta sound and mamogram done. The ulta sound doesn't bother me, but the machine press thing ... Bleh!

I'm positive all is fine, but, all good thoughts this way for a couple weeks, ok? ***smiles***

On the writing front, I got my 3rd short story finished, so only needing to finish the last one. Yay! Then, what's left is a quick check of how the Site's gonna look, and of course the editing of the stories. I'm still looking at March as the launch time. I feel like such a contradiction; all I want to do is write, I don't aspire to anything else, really, as far as a career or whatever, but, at the same time, it takes amazing amount of energy to get motivated to write. Laziness or apathy, I haven't decided yet. ***grins***

Everyone have an amazing weekend. And dont forget the ChatRoom on Sun Eves! That means you Girlfriend, and you know who you are. ***Grins***

Shirley ... Friday, Feb 13th ooohhhh ... bright and early; 8:00am EST

Well, the weekend is basically here, Yay! *grins* Harry and I are hoping to make it the science museum tomorrow. Still trying to finish my writing, and save money for going to my parents in April. Harry needs to get his car inspected next Month, so that's going to cost, I'm sure. It's not a new car by far. We both could use Optomatrist appointments too. It'll all get done, just one thing at a time. Hope everyone has a great weekend.

Shirley ... Jan. 23rd ... Approx 8:30pm EST

Hello to all, and Happy New Year. Better late than never, I suppose. *** grins ***
There honestly hasn't been too much going on lately, though. Hubby took me to
The Olive Garden last night, which was really sweet. One of the best parts of
going out like that is getting ready. I love the process of shaving, making sure the
nylons don't have runs in them, that the skirt and blouse are ironed. I like doing
makeup and my hair, cause I don't always bother. I don't feel I need foundation
and eyeliner when I'm going to Kroger for Diet Pepsi. *** chuckle *** Anyway, I
thought it was a great place. Reminded me alot of East Side Marios. There was
even plenty of leftovers for lunch today.

 I'm slowly finishing up the last 2 Short Stories I want to put on my Site. March is
still looking like the date, which I can live with. I'm nervous about it all going
smoothly. There are so many things that can mess up when you're sending
attachments to people, and I want to guarantee 24 hr delivery of the Stories. I have
a good Month and a half to work out any possible bugs though.

I'm still in the process of getting my Green Card and the paper work I need to get an SSN. I can't work without an SSN, so ...but, my extra time, I think at least, is being generally put to good use. Writing can almost take priority now, and even the

Hubby says that's where my focus should be right now, while it can be. It's going to be harder once I start working. Feels good to think that someone may be watching over me, and giving me the opportunities I need. Not that I'm very religious. Some people say life what you make it, so, here's my belate NeW Years cheer: "Here's to Making It!" *** Clinks a couple Diet Pepsi cans together. *** Hope 2004 is a blessed year for everyone.

Shirley ... Jan. 18th 2004 ... Approx 1:30pm EST

BIG THINGS in LITTLE PACKAGES

POEMS

SHIRLEY HITER 81

STORM CLOUDS

I shiver,
There's nothing to warm me.
A heart so cold and barren,
A mind without inspiration.

Storm Clouds are all I see.

My thirsty soul,
Desires to be fed.
I have nothing to nourish me,
My future, I can only dread.

Storm Clouds are all I see.

Partly my fault,
But I'll blame everyone else instead.
I need a reason to hold on,
My Faith hangs by a thread.

SHIRLEY HITER 82

CRAVINGS

Confessions of desire.
Admissions of a hunger,
Never satiated.
A thirst needing to be quenched.

I've tried to avoid this,
Perpetual arousal.
No chance of ignoring,
This constant yearning.

A love that doesn't allow,
Time for sleep.
An addiction beyond,
The want of redemption.

MUSINGS

Journey to you,
Somehow feeling blue.
Not wanting to cry,
Need to ask the question why.

Disbelieving I'm wrong,
Trying to be strong.
Focusing on me,
Unwilling to see.

In search of a solution,
Ridding myself of emotional pollution.
Ready to wager,
On a sweeter savor.

WHY?

Remind me of why,
I ever tried to fly.
Should have been told,
That the World has grown cold.

Wanting to be strong,
Trying to belong.
Weary of my tired mind,
Feeling like I'm just biding my time.

Giving up on aspiration,
Foregoing determination.
Fate is a delusion,
A damn cruel illusion.

WISHES

Waiting,
For my life to begin.
For some news,
To make me happy again.

Wanting,
To enjoy waking up.
The smells of,
A World alive.

Needing,
Someone to hold.
A partner,
Sharing thoughts and desires.

LIFE

Desire washed away,
Not wanting to stay.
I used to believe
Peace now hard to conceive.

Tired of this need to cry,
Just need to see the blue sky.
Fresh air and sunlight,
To make everything alright.

Love is fleeting,
Faith left me disbelieving.
Feeding off strife,
Mourning my life.

SO CLOSE

So close,
I can almost taste you.
A World of independence,
Waiting outside my door.

My desire grows,
Wonder if I'll ever truly know.
The cost of self reliance,
And the pleasure of defiance.

Freedom is inevitable,
I've waited for so long.
I longingly reach out,
Visions of peace are uncontained.

PENDING DESTINATION

Would you take me in
If I flew to you?

Swiftly, gracefully, soaring,
Would I traverse the skies.

I yearn for what my soul desires
A spark to light my love afire

Tell me how to reach you.
Tell me how to make you care.

Draw me a map, and I will find a way,
To ride the wind ...
To be on my way ...

My destination is paradise.
My destination, inside you.

SHOW ME

Take me to your dreams,
Show me a way inside,
Let me share your every joy,
In our affections, you can reside.

Reveal to me your passions,
Show me the fantasies resting there,
Let me be the one to spark those desires,
A hunger I will gladly bear.

Allow me to love you,
Show me the ways of your heart,
Let our souls entwine,
Never to be brought apart.

DO YOU?

If I call out to you,
Will you know it's me?
Will my voice sound
Gently on your ears?

Should I cling to the hope,
Of one day being,
Cuddled beside you,
As you lay there dreaming?

Do you know what it is that makes me care?
Do you know what it is that makes me ache to be there?

There's no cure for this strong obsession,
I'll hold fast this new devotion.
Yours until you let me go,
God, don't you ever let me go.

MISCHEVIOUS THOUGHTS

Denizens of Hell,
By a lovers wishing well.
Making appetites reign,
Causing control to be refrained.

Abundant rapture,
With a souls capture.
The search for contentment.
In discarded raiment

You can roll the dice,
And make a tally of the price.
Feel free to play the game,
With no sense of shame.

IMAGININGS

Each passing day without you,
I wonder,
Will the memories ever fade?

Your laugh,
Your voice in the night,
The way you seemed to caress my name.

Things I cling to, things I long to forget,
The reasons I awake each morning, the reasons I cry myself to sleep each night,
The only explanation for the sudden emptiness in my heart.

There is no regret,
I would endure this again and again,
For just a measure of the warmth your spirit gave me.

But this is not goodbye,
Just a mere change in direction,
So I'll brush a kiss past your lips, and whisper I love you, a final time, before I
turn,
And start out on my way.

WHAT

What can you say,
When you can't walk away.

What can you do,
When you're always blue.

What can you feel,
When a touch seems surreal.

SHIRLEY HITER 94

WANTING / NEEDING

Wanting to fly,
Needing to know why.
Life gets unraveled,
Such a long road to travel.

Want to shine,
Needing you as mine.
Not caring in right or wrong.
Just trying to belong.

Wanting to release,
Needing the pain to cease.
Prepared for a revelation,
Awaiting the declaration

SHIRLEY HITER 95

The Unpleasant Poem

My thoughts skitter,
Across uneasy emotions.
Daring me to justify,
Making me testify.

Reason and logic,
Have no use in the dealings of love.
At least that's what I was told,
While my heart was being sold.

Trespass at will,
My soul is open to all.
Yet desperate for warmth and tenderness,
To replace all the bitterness.

WASTING TIME

Can't stand the illusion,
Tired of the delusion.
The lies have spread too far,
I fear there's no solution.

If I attempt to be honest,
For once kept a promise.
Maybe I'd feel more deserving,
Perhaps not so cautious.

No longer want you reading my mind,
Don't want you wasting your time.
Won't take your fucking sympathy,
Never asked you to be solely mine.

Just let me leave you go,
Let's not make this torture slow.
I'll start over like times before,
This love was never meant to grow.

Tell Me

Tell me where I'm heading,
Tell me where I've been,
Tell me things to make me sane again.

All my thoughts are askew,
All I do is think of you.
Not knowing enough to stop,
Knowing too much to continue.

Frightened of myself, and what I want from you.
Frightened you already know of the things I do.
Caught between rapture and pain,
A heart that no longer feels shame.

This is what I am.
This is what I do.
Still, I always think of you.

WHAT FOR?

Waiting,
Searching,
For something yet unknown.
Diligent,
Praying,
For the release of self.
Emoting,
Crying,
For the past I never lived.
The future I'll never see.
For the Faith I've yet to believe in.

Anger

Sorry for my anger,
Sorry for my rage,
But I know I'll explode,
If I'm kept inside this cage.

I've endured long enough,
I'm releasing all my pain.
I've found the strength to stand,
I'm giving up my shame.

Don't mistake it for arrogance,
Or call it trying to even the score.
Get used the fact,
I'm not a passive child anymore.

The demons are gone,
My thoughts are strictly mine.
There's no holding back.
I'm through with wasted time.

She

She hides at the entrance of peace,
Watching everyone enter in.
She brushes off a tear from her cheek,
And wonders if she'll ever find a way inside.

She hears a small voice urging her to listen,
And struggles to understand its meaning.
This voice begins to teach her.
Over time, her strength increases.

This voice tells her about confidence and acceptance.
She learns how to love, and to be loved.
The voice shows her why she should be proud.
She's taught to raise her head up high.

She still goes back to the entrance to watch.
She starts seeing new things.
The entrance is no longer so far away.
The voice tells her it's time.

She walks towards inner peace.
She remembers to look in the shadows.
She sees someone hiding there.
She takes the girl by the hand, and teaches her how to get inside.

She Tries

She looks at him,
Tries to read
The thoughts hidden in his eyes.

She talks to him,
Tires to embrace
The reassurance in his voice.

She touches him,
Tries to send
Desire to the center of his soul.

The loves him,
Tries fervently to be
His everything.

Revelations

Wait a minute,
Stop and think,
What this choice,
Has made you.

You destroyed a trust,
You killed my faith,
I hope you can see why,
I can't have you in my life.

I needed to mean more to you,
Now I need to be free,
You had your opportunity,
But this could never last.

So now we part,
Not on necessarily good terms,
Things can't be the same,
You have obviously viciously changed.

FACES

Yes I have one,
But it's always changing.
Making it hard to see who I am.
An unwilling chameleon.

I want to fall for you gently like a snow flake.
Care to catch me on your tongue?
Could you really care for someone like me?
Someone who would always be a stranger.

My blood can boil,
Then I'm purring like a kitten on your lap.
I'm afraid of the monster under my bed,
Yet I never back down from a fight.

My contradictions can't be helped.
The confusion becomes a drug.
Should I be saved, or left to fend for myself?
Whatever my destiny, I can't see it being dull.

INSIGHTS

Having a dream is a dangerous sport,
Whether to catch it, or to let it slip away.

Time is confusing; passing by so slowly for some,
Me - it chases at a run.

Wanting my inspiration to last my lifetime,
Yet fearing I'll be severed from my life-line.

Writing must be my destiny,
But my pen has run away from me.

Flowing like rain they used to be,
Now sentences have eluded me.

Not wanting to bribe or coerce,
But I'll pay dearly to whomever finds my talent first.

Relying on myself has taken too much time,
There's no help for writing the next line.

Time will tell if I've endured,
Beyond the survival of my written word.

YOUR OWN THOUGHTS

YOUR OWN THOUGHTS ...

BIG THINGS in LITTLE PACKAGES

BIG THINGS in LITTLE PACKAGES

SHIRLEY HITER 109

BIG THINGS in LITTLE PACKAGES

Made in the USA
Lexington, KY
18 April 2014